the extreme sports collection

snowboarding!

shred the powder

by Chris Hayhurst

rosen publishing group's
rosen central
new york

Published in 1999 by The Rosen Publishing Group, Inc.
29 East 21st Street, New York, NY 10010

First Edition

Library of Congress Cataloging-in-Publication Data

Hayhurst, Chris.
Snowboarding! Shred the powder / Chris Hayhurst. — 1st ed.
p. cm. — (The extreme sports collection)
Includes bibliographical references (p. 60) and index.
Summary: Introduces the sport of snowboarding, with advice for beginners on equipment, techniques, competition, and safety.
ISBN 0-8239-3010-6
1. Snowboarding Juvenile literature. 2. Extreme sports Juvenile literature. [1. Snowboarding.] I. Title. II. Series.
GV857.S57H39 1999
796.9—dc21 99-14813
CIP

Manufactured in the United States of America

contents

1 What's Extreme?

Let's get something straight: What's extreme to you might not be extreme to the next person. And what's extreme to that person might be tame to you. You see, the word "extreme" is relative. It means something different for everybody.

One thing everyone can agree on, however, is that when it comes to extreme sports, snowboarding—sort of a combination of skateboarding, skiing, and surfing—definitely qualifies. But even snowboarding has changed over time. Years ago if you even owned a snowboard, you were extreme. If you talked about snowboarding, you were living on the edge. You were extreme just because you were different.

catching air

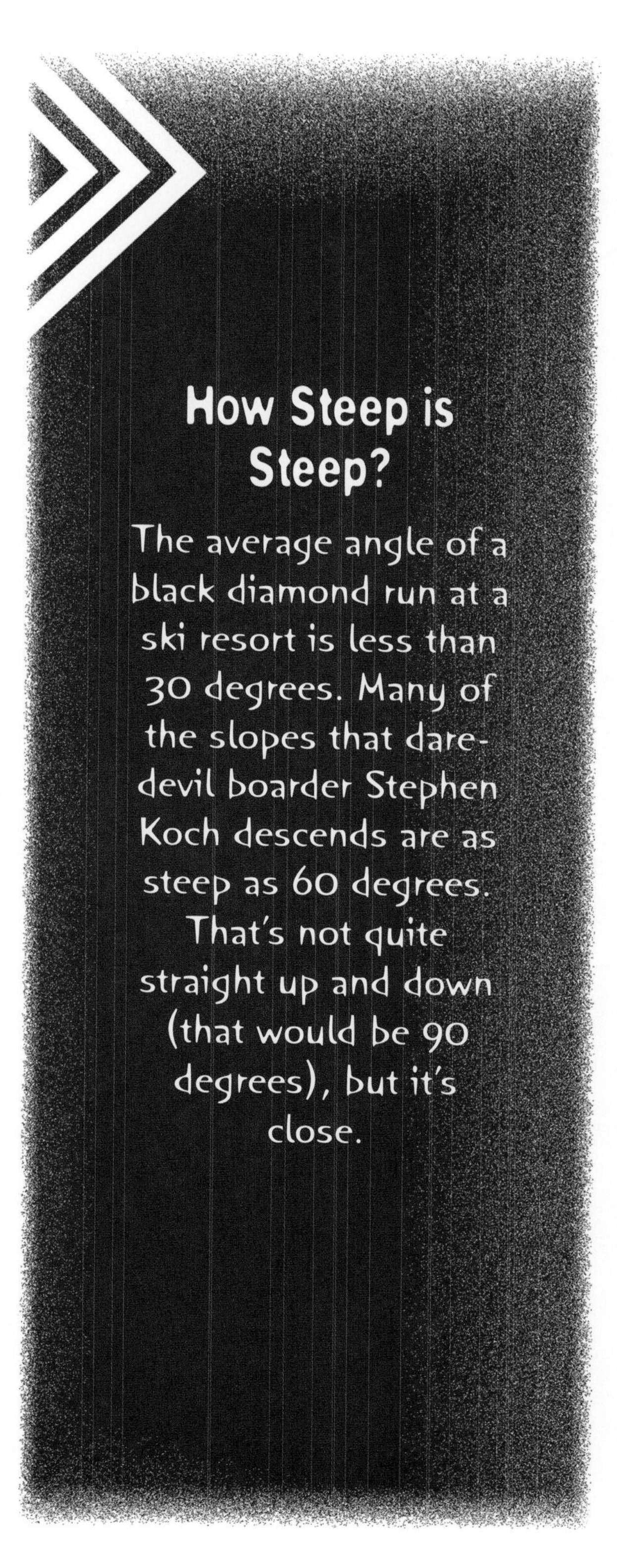

How Steep is Steep?

The average angle of a black diamond run at a ski resort is less than 30 degrees. Many of the slopes that dare-devil boarder Stephen Koch descends are as steep as 60 degrees. That's not quite straight up and down (that would be 90 degrees), but it's close.

Today it's not that simple. Millions of people snowboard. To be an extreme snowboarder nowadays, you not only need to have a snowboard, but you also have to know how to use it to do wild tricks. You have to know not only how to shred but how to shred fast. Really fast. You have to ride the steepest slopes, the deepest powder. Land the biggest jumps and the most spectacular twists. You have to be able to snowboard any stretch of snow out there and do it in style. That's extreme.

Now there are the X Games, a sort of miniature Olympics for extreme sports. Athletes from around the world gather for this event to show just how extreme they can be. They climb walls of ice; race down slippery, snow-covered ski slopes on mountain bikes; and jump out of airplanes with skateboards strapped to their feet. They compete to see who can grab the biggest air, who can hit the highest speeds, and who can perform the most difficult stunts. The winners are given gold

Boarder Bio

What does it take to be the king of the sky? Ask Jason Borgstede. Jason won the X Games Big-Air Competition by spinning around in the air two and a half times while holding on to the tail of his board. The trick's name? "900 Tail Grab," as in 900 degrees of rotation.

medals and the title of "Most extreme athlete on the planet." Most extreme, that is, until the next X Games, when new athletes will redefine what it means to be extreme.

Another version of extreme sports takes place behind-the-scenes, away from the glory that comes with television coverage and cheering crowds. These athletes prefer to play in the woods, alone with nature and the elements. They're the mountain climbers, the backcountry snowboarders

Boarder Bio

Stephen Koch, a "snowboard mountaineer" from Jackson Hole, Wyoming, is a true extreme athlete. He gets his kicks by climbing technically difficult routes up the world's biggest mountains, then strapping on his board at the summits and shredding down. He's planning on becoming the first human being to climb and ride the Seven Summits—the highest peak on each of the seven continents. Koch has already carved the steep, icy slopes of Aconcagua (22,834 feet) in the Andes Mountains of South America, Kilimanjaro (19,340 feet) in Africa, and Mount McKinley (20,320 feet) in Alaska. Next on his list is Mount Everest (29,028 feet), the highest peak in the world.

and skiers, the explorers. They'll never get a gold medal for what they do, and they probably wouldn't want one anyway. They're doing what they do because they love it, not because it attracts a crowd.

Most people agree that for a sport to be extreme, it has to be difficult—at least for the beginner. It must require specialized skills and techniques. It also requires an adventurous attitude—the kind of attitude that says there are no limits. Whether this means doing a flip off a halfpipe wall, blasting down the rocky chute of a remote mountain, or just getting on the chairlift for the first time all depends on who you are and what you're willing, or not willing, to try.

Extreme sports can be dangerous, but being extreme doesn't mean being foolish or taking unnecessary risks. No snowboarder wants to risk an injury that might mean never boarding again. You can be extreme and still follow safety rules.

If you think you want to be extreme but you're not sure where to start, try snowboarding. You'll find an adventure with every turn. With snowboarding, you can be as extreme as you want to be.

2 From Snurfers to Snowboards

Where It All Began

Snowboarding—a sport that began in the garages and backyards of creative thrill seekers looking for a new way to have fun—has come a long way over the years. In fact, since the invention of the snowboard in the mid-1960s, this sport has grown from a strange pastime that few people had tried or even heard about to one of the most popular winter activities in the world.

No one is sure who the first person was to come up with the idea of using a board to ride on snow. One of the first was an inventor named Sherman Poppen, who created the first

The earliest "snowboards" didn't look much like the ones we use today.

snowboard in 1965 after watching his daughter try to sled standing up. Combining the words "snow" and "surfer," he called his new invention a "snurfer." The snurfer was actually

just two skis screwed together. It didn't have bindings to hold the user's boots on to the board, and it didn't look much like today's snowboards, but it was very popular. Over the years millions of snurfers were sold.

Then in the early 1970s, a surfer and inventor named Dimitrije Milovich arrived on the winter sports scene. He designed a snowboard based on what he knew about surfboards. At the same time, a man named Bob Webber invented what he called a "skiboard" (not to be confused with today's extreme skiboards). Other people came up with similar inventions, and soon it seemed as if everyone was trying to develop the best board to handle the snow.

The breakthrough came in 1977. Jake Burton Carpenter, an inventor from Vermont, began fashioning snowboards out of wood. He attached rubber straps to the top of the board for bindings and coated the base of the board with polyethylene, or P-Tex. This slippery, flexible plastic allowed it to slide easily over the snow. Sleek, fast, small, and easy to turn, the first modern snowboard was born. And people loved it. Skiers, skateboarders, surfers, and others who wanted a new way to play in the snow took up snowboarding. Carpenter soon started a snowboard company called Burton.

In the spring of 1983, Carpenter staged the first National Snowboarding Championships in Snow Valley, Vermont. That same year a snowboard maker named Tom Sims organized the first-ever World Snowboarding Championships. Competitions were becoming popular, and boarders around the country were showing up to shred their stuff.

Other major competitions were held throughout the early 1980s in both the United States and Europe. Meanwhile Carpenter continued to improve his snowboards.

In 1988 the United States Amateur Snowboard Association (USASA) was formed, and in 1990 they held their first national championships in California. That same year Vail Ski Resort in Colorado opened a snowboard park, and the International Snowboard Federation (ISF) was formed. The ISF held its first official Snowboard World Championships in Austria in 1993.

That was a big year for snowboarding. There were more than fifty companies selling snowboards, and ESPN had just begun to televise the sport. Some people even hoped that snowboarding would make it into the 1994 Olympic Games as an official sport. That didn't happen. But snowboarding was a big hit at the Winter X Games (one of the first major extreme sports events), and its success convinced many people that it would someday become an Olympic event. Sure enough, in 1998 in Nagano, Japan, that

Extreme Fact

In 1986 Vermont's Stratton Mountain became the first resort to offer organized snowboarding instruction.

Olympic dream became a reality.

Today snowboarding equipment is constantly being improved. Riders are racing faster, jumping higher, and tackling harder terrain than ever before.

Extreme Fact

In 1985 only 7 percent of U.S. ski areas allowed snowboards. Today almost all areas allow boarders, and many offer halfpipes.

3 Boarding Styles

Not all snowboarding is the same. In fact, there are several different styles of snowboarding. Backcountry snowboarding takes place away from groomed trails and parks. Then there's freestyle boarding, in which riders launch themselves into the air and perform daring stunts. Some styles don't even require snow. If you like variety, snowboarding's your sport.

Most snowboarding occurs at one of three places: on ski trails at a mountain resort, at a snowboard park, or in the backcountry.

When riders stick to the slopes and trails of a ski mountain, they're freeriding. This type of snowboarding, which is very popular, is also called all-around or all-terrain. For a freerider nothing on the mountain is off-limits, and any kind of snow condition is fair game.

Freeriders can be found carving up the groomers, floating on deep powder, bouncing through the bumps, and weaving around the trees. Anywhere a lift can take them, they'll go. If you're a beginner, freeriding is the place to start. You'll get a good feel for the sport, and from there you can focus on more technical styles of boarding—like racing, for example.

Snowboard racing, also known as alpine boarding, takes place on the steep, groomed runs of a ski resort. Alpine boarders go for all-out speed and may enter competitive races. These competitions require them to weave down specially designed slalom courses at speeds sometimes topping sixty miles per hour. The boards they use are stiff and narrow and have long, sharp edges designed for difficult carving. If you've got plenty of snowboarding experience and you board for high-speed thrills, racing might be your ticket to the fast lane.

On the other hand, if air—as in catching air—is more your thing, you'd do better to try a different type of snowboarding: freestyle. This kind of boarding generally takes place at a snowboard park, an area at a ski resort that is made specifically for snowboarders. The main feature of a snowboard park is the halfpipe, and that's where you'll find boarders throwing

Extreme Gear: No snow? Get a MountainBoard!

This rubber-wheeled, all-terrain snowboard-skateboard combination allows slope-hungry shredders to rip during any season.

the really radical moves. The halfpipe, a U-shaped snow chute with high, curved walls, enables riders to become airborne several times during one run. This is where the best freestyle riders can be found, doing extreme acrobatic spins and twists that would impress even Michael Jordan.

Boarder Bio

Shannon Dunn

Birthday: November 26, 1972

Hometown: Steamboat Springs, Colorado

Shannon Dunn is one of the best female halfpipe shredders in the world. She's so good, in fact, that she even has her own custom-made snowboard—the "Shannon 44." The board is specially designed to help Shannon make smooth landings in the pipe—a difficult task when you make a habit out of launching yourself high into the air. Shannon even painted her own graphics on the board. A member of the U.S. Snowboard Team, Shannon finished fourth in the 1997 halfpipe World Championships.

Some people, however, prefer to get their snowboarding thrills away from the crowds. You can find—or try to find—these boarders in the backcountry. Backcountry boarding takes place in the mountains, away from the ski areas and the lift lines. Not many people backcountry snowboard, mainly because it's hard work.

Waiting for the Wind

One of the latest off-shoots of snowboarding involves wind power. In wind-snowboarding, riders rig sails to their snowboards and let the wind pull them across the slopes.

Up or Down?

Shredding down a mountain is certainly a blast, but what about climbing to the summit when there's no chairlift? Until recently, backcountry boarders had to wear snowshoes or slog through deep powder in their boots if they wanted to climb a mountain. But now a company called Voilà has come up with a better alternative: the Split Decision board. It's a snowboard that can be split in half to form two skis. After skiing up the mountain, all you have to do is snap the two boards together, and—voilà—you're ready to rip!

There's no such thing as a chairlift in the backcountry, and deep snow and harsh weather can make traveling difficult. But as any backcountry boarder will tell you, the sweat is worth it. When you've finally hiked, skied, or snowshoed to the top of a peak and have strapped on your board for the descent, all that work is quickly forgotten. On the way down, the only thing on your mind will be the powder beneath your board.

The 1998 Summer X Games in sunny San Diego, California

Big-Air at the X Games

Snowboarding has even hit the Summer X Games now! The Big-Air event takes place on a huge jump packed with artificial snow, and can be held anywhere, no matter what the climate.

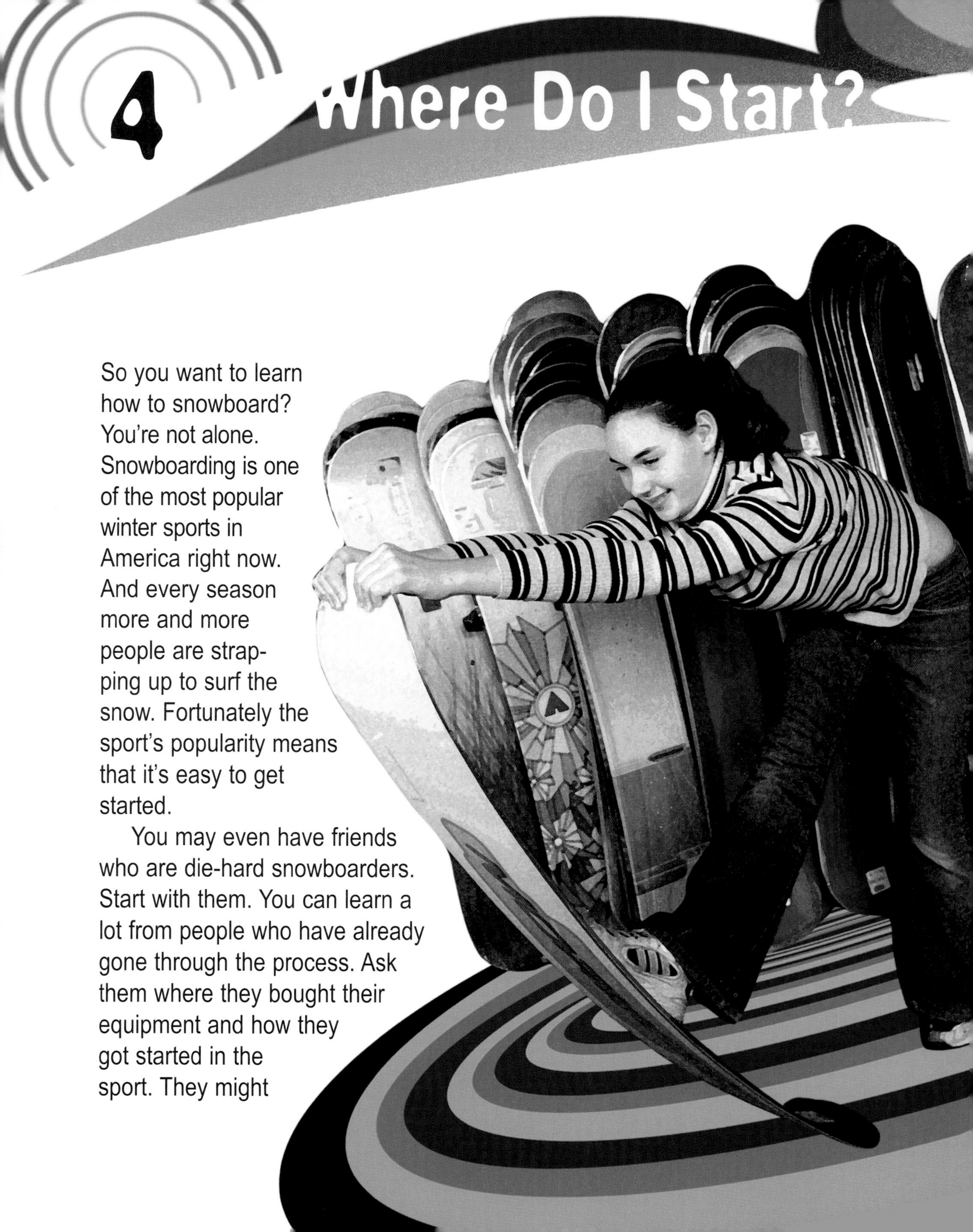

4 Where Do I Start?

So you want to learn how to snowboard? You're not alone. Snowboarding is one of the most popular winter sports in America right now. And every season more and more people are strapping up to surf the snow. Fortunately the sport's popularity means that it's easy to get started.

You may even have friends who are die-hard snowboarders. Start with them. You can learn a lot from people who have already gone through the process. Ask them where they bought their equipment and how they got started in the sport. They might even be willing to let you try out their boards.

If none of your friends snowboard, you'll have to start elsewhere. Check the phone book. Turn to the Yellow Pages and look up "Ski Equipment" or "Snowboard." If you live in or near a large or midsized town, you'll find a list of shops that sell new and used snowboarding gear. Most of these shops can offer good advice on where to snowboard in your area.

Boarding School

The best way to begin snowboarding is to take a lesson. It's the most important thing you can do to make sure that you get off to a good start. Your instructor will not only teach you the basic techniques and skills that you'll need to know in order to board, but will also give you equipment tips and important safety information. You'll learn how to get onto and off of the chairlift as well as how to control your board when your rear foot is out of the binding. You'll also find out if you're a goofy-footer (meaning that you ride with your right foot in front) or a regular-footer (with your left foot in front). In fact, most of your first lesson will probably be spent on the gentle "bunny slopes." Sounds wimpy, but don't worry. You'll have plenty of time later (when you know what you're doing!) to take on the hard stuff.

If you happen to live near a ski resort, you're in luck. Many resorts offer snowboarding lessons for all levels of ability, taught by instructors who have been certified by the Professional Ski Instructors of America (PSIA) or the American Association of Snowboard Instructors (AASI). You can expect a lesson to last anywhere from one hour to a full day or more. The price of approximately $55 to $75 per day usually includes the lesson, lift ticket,

Snowboard Patrol

Want to become a snowboard patroller? Contact your local resort's patrol director. If you're a good enough boarder, you may be hired to help patrol the mountain. If they're not hiring, ask if you can volunteer. You might even get a free season pass!

and rental equipment—which is a great deal if you're just starting out.

After your first lesson, you'll probably decide to devote the rest of your life to snowboarding. It's that addictive. At that point it's time to figure out what equipment you want to buy. You might already have a good idea of what you like just from the stuff you rented during the lesson. See chapter six for some other ideas on how to choose the best gear for you.

the 1998 Winter X Games in Crested Butte, Colorado

Once you have everything you need, you're officially ready to shred. Just remember, the skills aren't going to come easily at first, and it may take several lessons and an entire season of snowboarding before you finally get the hang of things. Just be patient and practice, practice, practice. And don't forget to have fun!

5 Safe Boarding

Snowboarding can be dangerous. Especially when you're hucking huge air off a jump or blasting down an icy slope at mach speed or, believe it or not, cruising soft powder in the backcountry.

The most important thing that you can do for your safety is to take a lesson from a certified instructor. The things you learn will help you to stay in one piece when you board. Practice what you learn on the open "bunny slopes." Once you've mastered the basics, you'll be ready to conquer the entire mountain.

Your equipment also plays a significant role in your safety. If you can rely on your gear to perform well, you can focus on other, more important things. First, have your snowboard and bindings tuned by a technician at the beginning of each season. Second, buy a helmet. The protection that the helmet will give your head in a crash could mean the difference between life and death. You should also wear wrist guards, especially when you're first learning to board. Finally, dress warmly in waterproof clothing. Staying dry will help prevent frostbite and hypothermia, a potentially life-threatening condition.

You'll probably make your very first turns at a ski resort. Most resorts ask boarders to follow a "responsibility code"—a list of rules endorsed by the National Ski Patrol that are designed to ensure your safety. Among other things, the code asks that you use a safety leash to prevent your board from getting away from you and endangering others. It also requires you to give those ahead of you the right of way and yield to others when you merge onto a trail. You should always observe any posted signs or warnings, and never ski or board in areas that are closed.

Backcountry snowboarding requires a few additional pieces of equipment and a much higher level of mental preparation. Avalanches, hidden boulders, cliffs, and trees

Fashion Tip:

To stay safe and look good, get a helmet. Some come with flexible horns or antlers, and others include funky designs and graphics.

Safety Tip:

Drink at least one liter of water per hour during strenuous boarding to avoid becoming dehydrated. If your body lacks the fluids it needs to function properly, you can become very sick.

Red

can all turn a great backcountry shred into a life-threatening nightmare. If you think you'll be exploring the backcountry, you should take a course in wilderness travel and avalanche safety. The American Avalanche Institute, most major outdoor stores, and the U.S. Forest Service all sponsor such courses. You also might be able to find a class sponsored by your local ski area or ski and snowboard shop.

Gear Tip:

The avalanche transceiver is no larger than a wallet, yet it's the most important piece of equipment you'll carry with you into the backcountry.

Don't try backcountry boarding on your own. Make sure you're with an adult who has backcountry experience and is carrying safety equipment, including an avalanche transceiver and probe (for rescuing someone trapped in an avalanche), a lightweight snow shovel, a first-aid kit, a map and compass, and extra clothing, water, and food. Everything can fit into a small backpack. Get a reliable weather report, and check the snow conditions before you go.

Last but not least, ski within your own personal limits. Don't push yourself beyond what you can handle, and you'll be sure to stay safe and injury-free.

6 Extreme Gear

Getting the Gear

All you need to start shredding are a board, boots, bindings, and something you probably have already—warm clothing.

Don't just go out and buy brand-new equipment. Gear is expensive and shouldn't be purchased until you know exactly what works best for you.

Borrow equipment from your friends and rent and test everything you can find until you're sure of what you like and what works well for you. Many snowboard shops will let you "demo" equipment, meaning that you pay a small fee to try out different brands of equipment. When you're done with the demo, you get your money back or a credit toward anything you decide to buy.

Once you're ready to buy, make sure that you go over your options. Gear can be expensive, so it's wise to shop around. Do you want new gear, or would you prefer to buy used equipment to save some money while you're still learning the ropes? Many towns have annual "ski swaps" where truckloads of winter gear, including snowboards, are bought and sold at low prices.

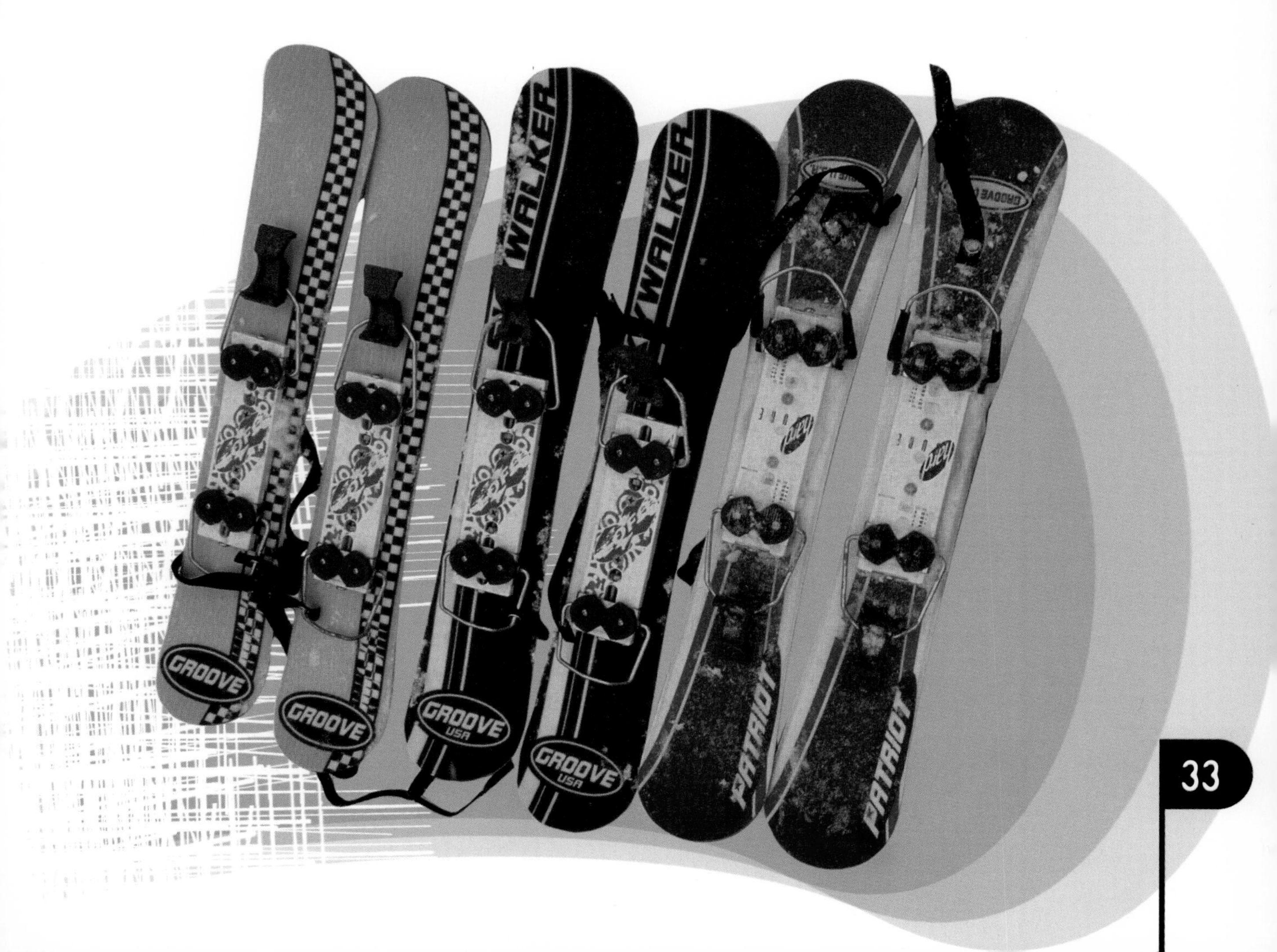

Board Basics

The most important piece of equipment for a snowboarder is—you guessed it—the board. Snowboards, which are getting lighter, stronger, faster, and tougher every season, are made up of several long strips of wood glued together and coated with plastic. The board's base is made of polyethylene or graphite and is waxed so that it glides well on snow. Steel edges allow riders to carve turns even in hard-packed snow or ice.

There are three main kinds of boards: Freerider boards are great for all-around shredding, powder surfing, and carving. Freestyle boards are

Gear Tip:

Boards range from under 100 cm to 180 cm in length. What size board should you use? It depends on your weight. You should be heavy enough to flex the board so that you can turn it and get big air.
You'll probably pay between $325 and $460 for a new beginner board. New boots and bindings will cost another $300. Used equipment costs significantly less—you could get everything you need for under $200.

designed primarily for tricks. The third kind of board is the alpine. It's designed for all-out speed.

There are a few things that you should know when shopping for a board. In general, the wider a board is, the harder it will be to steer. Flexible, or "soft," boards are easier for beginners to control than those that are stiff. A board with a specially designed side cut makes it easier to slice perfect half-circle turns. Twin-tip boards have

Word of the Day:

The plastic sheet that protects the top of a snowboard is made of acrylonitrile butadiene styrene. That's a mouthful, though, so you can call it ABS.

both tips turned up, whereas other boards have their front "uptipped" and their tail flat. Twin-tip boards are best for freeriding.

Finally, check out the board's colors and graphics—you want to surf the snow in style.

Footgear

The next thing you need is a good pair of boots. Snowboarding boots are different from regular winter boots. They're flexible but offer plenty of foot and ankle support. They're snug enough to let you feel the board and control it when you try to turn, but they're not so tight that your feet hurt.

There are two basic types of boots: soft and hard. Most boarders use soft boots. Lightweight and relatively inexpensive, they often come with a lace-up inner liner that helps support the lower calf, an important feature when you're leaning back to carve a turn. Soft boots that don't have this liner are designed for more advanced and freestyle riders.

Hard boots are used for racing and look like alpine ski boots. They have a plastic shell and are usually more expensive than soft boots.

Staying on Board

You've got a board. You've got boots on your feet. What's missing? The connector: bindings.

Bindings are mounted sideways on the snowboard and can usually be adjusted. There are two types of bindings: strap-ins and step-ins.

Most beginners use strap-in bindings. Also called soft bindings, they use a ratchet buckle system to cinch down the straps and fasten your boot tightly to the board. One strap loops over the toe and a second one goes over the instep (the middle part of your foot).

High-back plates on the bindings provide support for your lower legs as you turn, making edge control a breeze. Often a third strap wraps around the top of the high back to hold it snug against your leg.

Step-in bindings are the latest in hi-tech shredding gear. Metal plates mounted on the soles of your boots attach directly to brackets that are mounted on the snowboard. Forget about straps—you just clip your boots in and go!

What to Wear

Whoa! Don't go just yet! You forgot one last and very important thing—your clothes. Boarder clothes are like ski clothes, only a little baggier. Baggy is in. It's a fad, an attitude. (Or is that "altitude"?)

Make sure your clothes are lightweight, loose, comfortable, waterproof, and warm. Try wearing layers—a waterproof shell on the outside and a warm synthetic material like polypropylene or fleece on the inside. Your pants should have a padded seat. Leave your jeans at home.

Oh, and before you go, don't forget warm socks, goggles, a hat, and waterproof gloves. OK—now you can hit the slopes!

BURTON

7 Tips and Tricks

Snowboarding is not an easy sport to learn. But once you pick up the basic techniques, you'll probably find that the more difficult maneuvers—like how to catch air in the halfpipe or how to carve a turn on ice—come quickly. Before you know it, you'll be shredding so well that you'll think you were born to board.

But first you've got to master the "simple" stuff—the things you're taught at your first lesson. Like how to get on and off of the chairlift. And how to keep from falling down. And what you should do to keep from getting injured when you do fall.

You'll also begin to get a feel for the board and learn how to turn it effectively. Balance and your stance, combined with the ability to read the changing terrain, are the keys to a successful run. By bending your knees you weigh the board, which makes you turn. When you stand tall you unweigh the board, straightening your course. Whichever direction you shift your weight—toward your toe edge (for a frontside turn) or back to your heel edge (for a backside turn)—that's the direction you'll go.

When you're making a turn, your hand position is also very important. You should always keep your hands where you can see them, about three feet apart and level over the snow. Often all you have to do to change directions is point your hand the way you want to go. If all goes well, the rest of your body—and board—will follow.

Good! Now that you've got the basics down, it's time to learn a few tricks. What you do—if you can get the air—is limited only by your imagination.

Safety Tip:

When you fall, hold your elbows in and let your forearms absorb the impact. Try to avoid landing on your hands, as most injuries occur to the wrist and the fingers. If you fall backward, land on your butt, not your hands.

Always keep your head up and look straight ahead, in the same direction as your board is pointing. Oh, and try to keep your weight on your front foot when you make a turn!

Technique Talk

What's "fakie?" How about "sketching?" If you're new to boarding, you may have trouble keeping track of all the terms used to describe styles and tricks. Here's a short list to help you out.

Air to fakie: Hit a jump head-on, then turn in the air and land backward.

Alley-oop: Rotate 180 or more degrees in the uphill direction while in a halfpipe.

Backside air: Any airborne trick performed on the backside wall of a halfpipe.

Backside rotation: Rotating clockwise for a regular-footer, counterclockwise for a goofy-footer.

Big air: A high, long jump.

Bone: To emphasize a trick by straightening your arms and legs.

Duckfoot: To stand on a board with your toes pointing outward like a duck.

air to fakie

Fakie: Riding backward.

Grab: To grab your board with one or both hands while you're in the air.

Huck: To fly wildly through the air on your board, then crash.

Nose slide: To slide on the nose—the front tip—of the snowboard.

Revert: To switch between riding fakie and forward.

Sideslip: To slide or slip sideways down a hill while on your board.

Sketching: The act of nearly falling as you ride.

Switchstance: A trick performed while riding backward.

Tail wheelie: To ride on the board's tail while keeping its nose in the air.

grab

More advanced snowboarding techniques come with experience. You might even find yourself inventing your own tricks and maneuvers. The pros, who do tricks for a living, spend hours every day practicing the hardest moves. So don't expect to do anything too extreme until you've put in the time.

Tasty Tricks:

Take a bite out of one of these radical snowboarding tricks: chicken-salad air, eggflip, eggplant, fresh-fish air, mashed potato, McEgg, McTwist, pop tart, roast-beef air, spaghetti air, stale egg, stale fish, Swiss cheese air.

Who Are You Calling Goofy?

About half of all boarders ride "goofy-foot," with their right foot forward on the board. The other half ride "regular-foot," with their left foot in front. So who are you calling goofy?

8 Competition

After you've learned the basics of boarding, you may decide that you want to compete. Then again, you may not. Competing is not for everyone. Many people board throughout their entire lives and never enter one competition.

If you do want to put your skills to the test and have never done so before, the best place to start is at the nearest mountain. Ask the special-programs coordinator when the snowboarding events will be held, then find out if you can register to enter. You'll probably get to compete on the race-course or in the halfpipe against other boarders of similar age and ability.

Another place to begin is in school. Maybe you can start a snowboarding club or even a team. Competitions could be held between you and the other members of the club or between your team and those from other schools in your region.

If real competition is not your thing, try setting up a fun race or halfpipe showdown with your friends next time you're looking for something exciting to do at the resort.

Once you get a taste of competition, you may be hooked. Some boarders love the thrill of getting big air or ripping downhill at high speed before a screaming crowd of friends and fans.

Boarders compete on the halfpipe during the 1998 Winter X Games at Crested Butte, Colorado.

The Pros

It can also be fun to watch others compete, especially professionals. In the United States, the U.S. Amateur Snowboard Association (USASA) and U.S. Ski and Snowboard Association (USSA) sponsor major national competitions. Most of these competitions consist of several different events.

In the freestyle event, halfpipe riders launch monster air and perform spectacular flips and twists while the judges look on. In the downhill, or alpine, event, competitors speed down the mountain in the Super G event or carve turns around gates (flexible poles planted in the snow) in the slalom and giant slalom.

The X Games also stage what is called Boardercross, or Boarder X. In this thrilling event, several riders race down the slope at the same time thrashing moguls, drop-offs, and jumps. The first person down the mountain is the winner.

Extreme Fact:

The machine used to create the halfpipes at the 1998 Winter Olympics in Nagano, Japan, was called a "pipe dragon." The monstrous-looking vehicle used an enormous mechanical arm to smooth and groom the half-pipe walls to just the right height and angle.

Boarder Bio

Ross Powers
Birthday: February 10, 1979
Hometown: South Londonderry, Vermont

Introducing the best male halfpipe snowboarder in the United States: Ross has been shredding since he was a third-grader and has been winning all sorts of competitions ever since. In 1993 at the age of fourteen, Ross won the Junior National Snowboarding Championship. Three years later he won a gold medal in the halfpipe competition at the 1996 World Snowboarding Championships. In 1998 he won the slopestyle event at the Winter X Games. He's also been the USSA National Champion and was a member of the U.S. Snowboard Team at the 1998 Winter Olympics. There, to nobody's surprise, Ross won a bronze medal in the men's halfpipe event.

Snowboarding became an official Olympic sport in 1998, when boarders competed in alpine and freestyle. Now boarders from around the planet can show the world their best tricks every four years. The U.S. Snowboard Team is always looking for top competitors. Are you extreme enough to become an Olympian? The 2002 Winter Olympics will be held in Salt Lake City, Utah. See you there!

1998 Olympic Gold Medalists

Ross Rebagliati, Canada, Men's Slalom
Karine Ruby, France, Women's Slalom
Gian Simmen, Switzerland, Men's Halfpipe
Nicola Thost, Germany, Women's Halfpipe

X-planations

alpine Recreational downhill riding, usually at a ski resort.

avalanche probe A pole used by backcountry boarders to poke through the snow and help find buried avalanche victims.

avalanche transceiver An electronic device used by backcountry boarders to locate missing avalanche victims.

backcountry snowboarding Snowboarding on ungroomed trails or in the woods.

backside The side of the snowboard where the rider's heels rest.

backside turn A right turn for a regular-footer; a left turn for a goofy-footer.

base The bottom of a board, usually made of polyethylene, or P-Tex.

bonk To hit an object with your snowboard as you fly over it.

carve To turn using the board's edges.

dehydration A condition that occurs when a person doesn't drink enough water.

face plant To fall on your face.

freeride Riding all over a mountain, on any terrain.

freestyle Riding that includes tricks and maneuvers.

freshies Fresh powder snow.

frontside The side of the board where the rider's toes rest.

frontside turn A left turn for a regular-footer; a right turn for a goofy-footer.

frostbite A condition in which parts of the body (usually fingers or toes) become frozen.

goofy-footer Someone who rides with the right foot forward.

groomers Trails at a ski resort that are groomed to be smooth and clear.

halfpipe A U-shaped chute with high, curved sides used to catch air and perform tricks while freestyle boarding.

hypothermia A dangerous condition in which the body's temperature drops well below normal.

jib To ride on something other than snow, like a trash can or a bench.

leash A safety strap attached to a rider's front foot and used to keep the snowboard from sliding away.

lip The top edge of the halfpipe wall.

moguls Jumps on a snowboard trail.

nose The front tip of the snowboard.

pow Short for "powder snow."

quarter pipe A halfpipe with only one wall.

regular-footer Someone who rides with the left foot forward.

shred To board like a pro; to "rip" or "jam."

shred stick The snowboard.

sick Cool; rad.

side cut The way a board's edge curves toward the board's center.

slalom A zigzagging downhill course or race past flags or other obstacles.

slopestyle Another name for freestyle boarding.

stance The way you stand on a board.

tail The rear tip of the board.

twin-tip A board designed for freestyle snowboarding with an identical tip and tail so that it may be ridden in either direction.

unweigh To take pressure off of the board with your legs.

weigh To press down on the board with your legs.

Extreme Info

For more information about snowboarding, check the following organizations.

American Association of Avalanche Professionals
P.O. Box 1032
Bozeman, MT 59771
(406) 587-3830
e-mail: avalpro@theglobal.net
Web site: http://www.avalanche.org/~aaap/

American Association of Snowboard Instructors
133 South Van Gordon Street, Suite 102
Lakewood, CO 80228
(303) 987-2700
e-mail: aasi@aasi.org
Web site: http://www.aasi.org

American Avalanche Institute
P.O. Box 308
Wilson, WY 83014
(307) 733-3315
e-mail: aai@wyoming.com

Canadian Ski Association
1600 James Naismith Drive
Gloucester, ON K1B 5N4
e-mail: canski@agt.net

National Ski Patrol
133 South Van Gordon Street, Suite 100
Lakewood, CO 80228
(303) 988-1111
Fax: (303) 988-3005
e-mail: nsp@nsp.org
Web site: http://www.nsp.org

United States Amateur Snowboard Association (USASA)
P.O. Box 3927
Truckee, CA 96160
(530) 587-6656
e-mail: office@usasa.org
Web site: http://www.usasa.org

U.S. Ski and Snowboard Association (USSA)/U.S. Ski and Snowboard Team
P.O. Box 100
Park City, UT 84060
(435) 649-9090
e-mail: special2@ussa.org
Web site: http://www.ussa.org

Web Sites

About Snowboarding!
http://www.aboutsnowboarding.com

Adventure Time
http://www.adventuretime.com

Always Riding
http://www.alwaysriding.com

BoardZ Online Magazine
http://www.boardz.com

Cyberspace Snow and Avalanche Center
http://www.csac.org

ESPN/Extreme Sports
http://espn.go.com/extreme

ESPN/X Games
http://espn.go.com/xgames/winterx98/snowboard/index.html

Extreme Sports On-line
http://www.extreme-sports.com

Faceshot
http://www.faceshot.com

GreatOutdoors.com
http://www.greatoutdoors.com/snowboarding/index.htm

Mountain Zone
http://www.mountainzone.com/snowboarding/index.html

Ski Central
http://skicentral.com/snowboarding.html

Snowboarding Online
http://www.solsnowboarding.com

Snowlink
http://www.snowlink.com

Snowsports Resource Guide
http://www.snowsportsresource.org

Where to Play

Camps and Schools

To find a snowboarding camp near you, contact the United States Amateur Snowboarding Association. Here are a few to get you started:

Craig Kelly's World Snowboard Camp
P.O. Box 5090
Glacier, WA 98244
(360) 599-1258

High Cascade Snowboard Camp
P.O. Box 6622
Bend, OR 97708
(800) 334-4272 or (541) 389-7404
e-mail: highcascade@highcascade.com
Web site: http://www.highcascade.com

Mount Hood Snowboard Camp
P.O. Box 140
Rhododendron, OR 97049
(503) 668-8322
Web site: http:www.snowboardcamp.com

School of Snowboarding
P.O. Box 66
Invermere, BC V0A 1KO
Canada
(250) 342-6941 or (888) SOS-7799 [767-7799]
Fax: (250) 342-3727
e-mail: info@skischool.com
Web site: http://www.skischool.com

Superpipe Snowboard Camp
5-2704 Cheakamus Way
Whistler, BC V0N 1B2
Canada
(604) 938-2476
email: csm@whistlernet.com
Web site: http://www.superpipe.org

U.S. Snowboard Training Center
P.O. Box 360
Brightwood, OR 97011
(800) 325-4430

Windell's Snowboard Camp
P.O. Box 628
Welches, OR 97067
(800) 765-7669
e-mail: windcamp@teleport.com
Web site: http://www.windells.com

Competitions

There are countless amateur snowboarding competitions held in the United States and Canada throughout the year, and many professional competitions also hold amateur events. Contact the USASA or check your favorite snowboarding zine for more information on dates and details.

The best-known professional competitions are, of course, the Winter X Games and the Winter Olympics. The Winter X Games take place annually, and the Winter Olympics are held every four years. The ISF holds international championships in alpine and halfpipe (freestyle) each year. Other major pro events include the U.S. Grand Prix, the Vans Triple Crown, the Timberline Classic, the American Snowboard Tour, and the Swatch Boardercross Tour. Many of the Web sites listed in Extreme Info have schedules and calendars of both pro and amateur competitions.

Extreme Reading

Bennett, Jeff, and Scott Downey. *The Complete Snowboarder.* Camden, ME: Ragged Mountain Press, 1994.

Eubanks, Steve. *I Know Absolutely Nothing About Snowboarding.* Nashville, TN: Rutledge Hill Press, 1997.

Hart, Lowell. *The Snowboard Book.* New York: W.W. Norton & Co., 1997.

Jay, Jackson. *Snowboarding Basics.* Danbury, CT: Children's Press, 1996.

Lurie, John. *Fundamental Snowboarding.* Minneapolis, MN: Lerner Publications Co., 1996.

McKenna, Lesley. *The Fantastic Book of Snowboarding.* Brookfield, CT: Copper Beech Books, 1998.

Reichenfeld, Rob, and Anna Bruechert. *Snowboarding.* Champaign, IL: Human Kinetics Publications, 1995.

Ryan, Kevin. *The Illustrated Guide to Snowboarding.* Indianapolis, IN: Masters Press, 1998.

Ryan, Pat, and Bill Lund. *Extreme Snowboarding.* Mankato, MN: Capstone Press, 1998.

Sullivan, George. *Snowboarding: A Complete Guide for Beginners.* New York: Puffin Books, 1997.

Magazines

Couloir
P.O. Box 2349
Truckee, CA 96160
(530) 582-1884
e-mail: couloir@telis.org
Web site: http://www.couloir-mag.com

Mountain Zone
1415 Western Avenue #300
Seattle, WA 98101
(206) 621-8630
e-mail: info@mountainzone.com

Powder
P.O. Box 58144
Boulder, C0 80320
(800) 289-8983
e-mail: powdermag@surferpubs.com

Ski
P.O. Box 55532
Boulder, CO 80322
(800) 678-0817
Web site: http://www.skinet.com/ski

Ski Canada
35 Riviera Drive, Bldg. 17
Markham, ON L3R 8N4
(800) 263-5295
Web site: http://www.skicanadamag.com

Snowboard Canada
2255B Queen Street East, Suite 3266
Toronto, ON M4E 1G3
Canada
(800) 223-6197
e-mail: subscriptions@snowboardcanada.com

Snowboarder
P.O. Box 1028
Dana Point, CA 92629
(800) 955-9120
e-mail: snwbrdrmag@surferpubs.com
Web site: http://www.snowboardermag.com

Snowboard Life
P.O. Box 469009
Escondido, CA 92046
(760) 745-2809 or (888) TWS-MAGS [897-6247]
Web site: http://www.twsnow.com

TransWorld Snowboarding
P.O. Box 469019
Escondido, CA 92046-9019
(760) 745-2809 or (888) TWS-MAGS [897-6247]
Web site: http://www.twsnow.com

Index

Credits

About the Author

Chris Hayhurst is a freelance writer and photographer who specializes in the outdoors, sports, and environmental issues. In his spare time, he enjoys hiking, rock climbing, telemark skiing, and anything that takes him into the backcountry. He lives in Santa Fe, New Mexico.

Photo Credits

Cover photo TK; p. 2, Allsport USA; p. 4, Nathan Bilow; pp. 6, 18, International Stock ©Tony Demin; pp. 8,10, Allsport/Vandystadt; p. 9, International Stock ©Peter Kinninger; pp. 12, 15, 44, Allsport/Mike Powell; pp. 13, 16, 24–25, 37, 48, 50, Nathan Bilow/Allsport US; pp. 14, 28, 31, 35, 46, 47 Agence Vandystadt; p. 19, Ezra O. Shaw/Allsport; pp. 20, 21, 32, 33, 39, by Thaddeus Harden; p. 23, International Stock ©Kirk Anderson; pp. 26, 40, 43, 45, International Stock ©Eric Sanford; p. 29, Jed Jacobsohn/Allsport; p. 30, Vandystadt/Allsport USA; p. 34, Harry How/Allsport; p. 36, Jamie Squire/Allsport.
Thanks to the Princeton Ski Shop in Manhattan for allowing us to shoot the photos on pages 20, 21, 32, 33, and 39 in their store.

Design and Layout

Oliver H. Rosenberg

Consulting Editor

Amy Haugesag